# YEAR 4

# PARTNER GAMES

Patsy F. Kanter
*and*
Janet G. Gillespie

*with revisions by*
Ann Montague-Smith

Nelson

## CREDITS

Cover: Betsy Everitt
Pencil Drawings: Martha Weston
Illustrations: Shelley Mathers
Electronic Art: PC&F, Inc.
Editor: Mairi Sutherland
Revisions typeset by: Pentacor PLC, High Wycombe, Bucks, UK

**Revised edition © 1999 Thomas Nelson & Sons Ltd.**
**First edition © 1998 Great Source Education Group, Inc.**

**Thomas Nelson & Sons Ltd**
Nelson House
Mayfield Road
Walton-on-Thames
Surrey
KT12 5PL

Thomas Nelson is an International Thomson Company

Published by Thomas Nelson & Sons Ltd 1999
ISBN 0-17-430053-0
9 8 7 6 5 4 3 2 1
03 02 01 00 99
Printed in China

All rights reserved. No part of this publication may be reproduced, copied or transmitted in any form or by any means, electronic or mechanical, including photocopy, recording, or any publisher or under licence from the Copyright Licensing Authority Ltd, 90 Tottenham Court Road, London W1P 9HE

The publisher grants permission for copies of the copymaster pages (22–31) to be made without fee as follows:

Private purchasers may make copies for their own or for use by their own students; school purchasers may make copies for use within and by the staff and students of the institution only. This permission to copy does not extend to additional institutions or branches of an institution, who should purchase a separate master copy of the book for their own use.

For copying in any other circumstances, prior permission must be obtained in writing from Thomas Nelson and Sons Ltd.

# INTRODUCTION

*Partner Games* consists of a series of books for Reception to Year 6, England and Wales, P1 to P7 in Scotland. Within each book there are twenty-one numeracy games for two players. The games are designed to offer children opportunities to:

▶ develop new number concepts and practise those they have already acquired;

▶ talk about their mathematics with their partner, working collaboratively;

▶ use and develop their ability to solve problems and to identify and try possible winning strategies;

▶ develop their ability to record their mathematics using numerals and symbols.

## The National Curricula for England and Wales

The activities support parts of the Programmes of Study for Key Stage 2. For each activity, the recommended age and teaching objectives are specified so that the activities can be used as part of the school's planned scheme of work. The table below shows the curriculum coverage, using the strands from the National Numeracy Strategy.

## Mathematics Curriculum Coverage for England and Wales

| Strands from the Numeracy Strategy | Activity pages |
| --- | --- |
| **Numbers and the number system** | |
| Place value, ordering and rounding | 4, 5, 10, 20 |
| Fractions and decimals | 13, 15, 16, 17, 18 |
| **Calculations** | |
| Rapid recall of addition and subtraction facts | 21 |
| Pencil and paper procedures (+ and −) | 11 |
| Mental calculation strategies (× and ÷) | 20 |
| Understanding multiplication and division | 8 |
| Rapid recall of multiplication and division facts | 3, 9, 12, 14 |
| **Making sense of problems** | |
| Reasoning about numbers or shapes | 7, 19 |
| Problems involving 'real life' or money | 1, 2, 6 |

Partner Games: Year 4

## The Daily Mathematics Lesson

These activities are intended to be used with pairs of children, as part of the main teaching and pupil activities. The activities can be used with children working in pairs to:

▶ target pairs for developing particular concepts or skills;
▶ extend previous work;
▶ offer challenge, to encourage children to use their mathematical understanding in problem-solving situations;
▶ encourage discussion and cooperation between the children.

The activities can also be used with groups working in pairs at the same activity, with the support of an adult who:

▶ helps to develop new mathematical language through discussion;
▶ encourages appropriate recording of mathematical outcomes;
▶ assesses understanding of new concepts and vocabulary;
▶ gives feedback to individuals, reflecting the quality of their ideas.

## National Guidelines for Scotland: Mathematics 5–14

The activities in the book support some aspects of the Attainment Outcomes and Targets for P4, levels B and C, as shown in the table below.

## Mathematics Curriculum Coverage for Scotland

| Attainment Targets and Strands | Activity pages |
| --- | --- |
| **Problem-solving and enquiry** <br> Starting a task; doing a task; reporting on a task | 7, 19 |
| **Number, money and measurement** <br> Range and type of numbers <br> Money <br> Add and subtract <br> Multiply and divide | 4, 5, 10, 13, 15, 16, 17, 18, 20 <br> 16 <br> 2, 11, 21 <br> 2, 3, 8, 9, 12, 14, 20 |

## How to use the book

Using the relevant Mathematics Curriculum Coverage table, find an activity which supports your planning. The specific teaching objective (Focus), and age recommendation, is given on each activity page to help you to make that choice. You may decide to choose a range of activities to support differentiation in your class, with each ability group working, in pairs, at a specific activity.

The resources needed for the games are those available in all schools. These are listed inside the back cover of this book, and include counters, coins (real or plastic), calculator, base ten apparatus such as Dienes blocks, and number dice (or use a plain one and write the numerals on it). There is a pack of Fraction/Decimal Cards which is available from Nelson Customer Services (Tel. 01264 342 995/996; Fax. 01264 342 788), order reference number ISBN 0-17-430074-3 (single deck); ISBN 0-17-430076-X (pack of 3 decks).

Some activities have game boards. These can be photocopied, then placed inside plastic sleeves. A piece of A4 card inside the sleeve will help to keep the game board rigid.

## How to support learning

Before the players begin their game, emphasise the rule that they must explain to their partner what their accumulated total is before they toss the dice or draw the next card and how much more they need in order to win. This will help them to practise counting, totalling, and using mental strategies to calculate throughout the game.

Where children are asked to keep a written record, encourage them to say out loud what they are writing. This helps them to read the mathematical sentence, and to interpret numerals and symbols.

## How to introduce the game

If all the children in the class will play the game (over time) introduce the game during a whole class session. Play the game, with you playing against the class. It may help to keep the children's attention by using the overhead projector to show the game. If this is not possible, and there is a game board for the game, consider enlarging the board to A3 so that everyone can see it clearly.

If the game will be used by a group, or just one pair, then introduce the game in the same way, with you playing against those children.

Model the way of working by explaining each step that you take. Say out loud how much you have accumulated, and what you will need to win. Encourage the children to do the same. When they are confident of how the game works, they can then play in their pairs. If another adult will work with a group, make sure that they have understood the purpose of the game, and read the instructions.

Each game should be played several times by the children, as the outcome will be different each time. This will encourage them to feel confidence in their improving numeracy skills and problem-solving ability, and, of course, give them more opportunities to win!

## Assessment

Listen in as the children play the games. This will offer opportunities to observe whether they have understood the concept or can use the skill associated with the game. Where children give wrong responses during the game, this may well give useful insights into misconceptions. Many of the games have assessment tips. These, together with the Focus (from the teaching objectives of the Numeracy Strategy), will help to identify individuals' strengths, where there is a need for further teaching because of misunderstanding, and where further challenge would be appropriate.

## Working with parents and carers

Many of these games can be used as 'homework'. Check that the materials required are those readily available at home, or have loan sets available. Photocopy the relevant game instruction page and send home as part of the school's homework strategy. The Focus of the game is on the sheet so that those at home will understand its purpose.

Parents and carers may appreciate the opportunity to use these games as part of a home–school link evening for mathematics. This would offer opportunities for them to play the games with teachers, and understand how to help their children develop their understanding and use of mathematical language.

# Try for £1.00

## Materials
Real coins or play money (1p, 2p, 5p, 10, 20p and 50p coins), one 1–6 number dice, paper

## Directions
The goal is to get as close to £1.00 as possible without going over. Each player prepares a recording sheet as shown. Players take turns tossing the dice and deciding whether to take that number in pennies, 2p, 5p, 10p, 20p or 50p coins. A player records the choice of coins, then adds these coins to his or her collection, making exchanges whenever possible. The player then announces and records the new total. Players must trade up to the next coin whenever possible. After six tosses, the player with an amount closer to £1.00 without going over wins.

## Variations
1. Set £2.00 as the goal to reach.
2. Set £10 as the goal.

## Focus
▶ Use all four operations to solve word problems involving money, using one or more steps, including converting pounds to pence and vice versa.

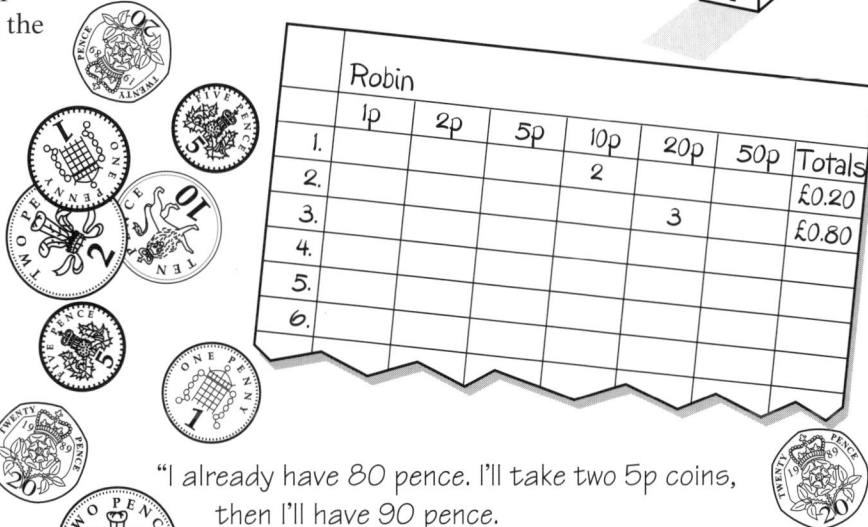

| | Robin | | | | | | |
|---|---|---|---|---|---|---|---|
| | 1p | 2p | 5p | 10p | 20p | 50p | Totals |
| 1. | | | | | | | |
| 2. | | | | 2 | | | £0.20 |
| 3. | | | | | 3 | | £0.80 |
| 4. | | | | | | | |
| 5. | | | | | | | |
| 6. | | | | | | | |

"I already have 80 pence. I'll take two 5p coins, then I'll have 90 pence."

## Assessment Tips:
▶ After playing a few times, is the child using mental addition to predict the consequences of taking specific coins?
▶ Can the child easily count mixed coins?

Partner Games: Year 4

# Go for it — I've got it!

## Materials
0–9 numeral cards

## Directions
One player shuffles the numeral cards and places 5 cards face up in a row. One card from the deck is turned up. The object of the game is to be the first player to use the numbers on all five cards to make a number sentence whose solution is equal to the face up target card. Most players will choose to use addition and subtraction but multiplication and division may be allowed. As soon as a player has a solution, the player says, "I've got it!" and **explains his or her solution.**

If neither player can create an expression with a solution equal to the face up card, another card is turned over from the deck until someone has a solution.

Reshuffle all cards into the pack before starting the next round.

## Variations
1. To change the game, use cards 0–5.
2. Place a time limit on creating an appropriate expression before drawing another card.

## Focus
▶ Use all four operations to solve word problems involving numbers in 'real life', using one or more steps.

6

4  9  3  0  1

"I've got it!
$(9 \div 3) + (4 - 1) + 0 = 6$."

### Assessment Tips:
▶ Does the child demonstrate perseverance using the guess-and-check problem-solving strategy?
▶ Does the child demonstrate facility with basic facts?

# FACT COMPARING

## MATERIALS
0–9 numeral cards

## DIRECTIONS
Each player shuffles a set of Numeral Cards and places them face down on the table. Players each turn over two cards and multiply the two numbers on their cards. **Each player states his or her multiplication fact.** (Six times seven, or six groups of seven, is forty-two.) The player with the greater product keeps all four cards. In the case of a tie, players each turn over two more cards and multiply again until the tie is broken. After all the cards are used, the player with more cards wins the game.

## VARIATIONS
1. For an easier game, sort the cards into two packs, 0–4 and 5–9. Each player turns over one card from each pack and multiplies the two numbers.
2. To increase the challenge, use only the 4–9 cards.
3. Players each draw three cards, keep two and compare the products.

## FOCUS
▶ Know by heart multiplication facts for 2, 3, 4, 5 and 10 times-tables.
▶ Begin to know multiplication facts for 6, 7, 8 and 9 times-tables.

## ASSESSMENT TIP:
▶ Is the child recalling the multiplication facts? If not, what strategies is the child using?

# TARGET NUMBER

### MATERIALS
One 1–6 number dice, base 10 apparatus such as Dienes blocks, paper, calculator (optional)

### DIRECTIONS
The object of the game is to be the first player to build two of the target numbers listed below. If needed, players create place value mats as shown.

Players begin by agreeing on two target numbers. The object of the game is to be the first player to build both numbers without going over. Players take turns rolling the dice. The player decides to take that number in thousands, hundreds, tens, or ones. A player may choose to divide this amount between the target numbers. When a player has ten ones they must be exchanged for a ten. Ten tens must be exchanged for one hundred, and ten hundreds for one thousand. A player who cannot use the number tossed loses the turn. Before tossing the dice each time, the player says **the number accumulated.**

### VARIATION
Select one or three target numbers.

Target Numbers – Pick Two
1245   843   690
508   1177   1003

**Place Value Mats**

| Thousands | Hundreds | Tens | Ones |
|---|---|---|---|
|  |  |  |  |
| Thousands | Hundreds | Tens | Ones |
|  |  |  |  |

---

### ASSESSMENT TIPS:
- Does the child develop strategies for choosing a denomination and distributing the value?
- Does the child demonstrate clear understanding of place value?
- Does the child show facility with addition and subtraction?

---

### FOCUS
- Read and write numbers to at least 10,000 in figures and words; know what each digit represents and partition numbers into thousands, hundreds, tens and ones (Th H T U).

# Number Comparing

## Materials
0–9 numeral cards, 5 counters, paper

## Directions
The object of the game is to create and compare 4-digit numbers that are as large as possible.

The Numeral Cards are spread out face down. Each player draws five cards and arranges them into a four-digit number of the greatest value, discarding the card that seems least helpful. After both numbers are created, the players **read the numbers using the language of comparison (five thousand, four hundred and twenty-one is greater than four thousand, two hundred and ten).** The numbers are recorded on the paper, using the <, >, and = symbols.

The player who created the larger number receives a counter. At the end of five rounds, the player with more counters wins.

## Variations
1. The player with the smaller number receives a counter.
2. Children draw more cards and create larger numbers. They always draw one more card than they need.

## Focus
▶ Use, read and write the vocabulary of comparing and ordering numbers; use correctly symbols such as <, >, =; give one or more numbers lying between two others and order a set of whole numbers with up to four digits.

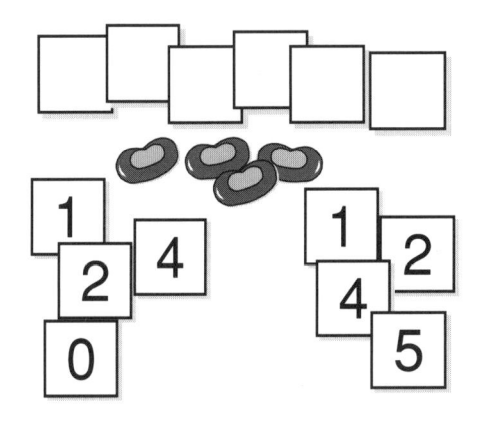

"My 5421 is greater than 4210. I get a bean."

| | Ian | | Zoe |
|---|---|---|---|
| 1 | 3120 | > | 1926 |
| 2 | 4210 | < | 5421 |
| 3 | | | |
| 4 | | | |
| 5 | | | |

## Assessment Tips:
▶ Is the child able to demonstrate number sense in creating the larger number?
▶ Can the child correctly read a 4-digit number?

Copyright © Thomas Nelson and Sons Ltd 1999

**Partner Games: Year 4**

# Pocket money

## Materials
Real coins or play money (1p, 2p, 5p, 10p, 20p and 50p coins), 0–9 numeral cards, 5 counters

## Directions
The object of the game is to create a specific amount of money using the fewest coins. The Numeral Cards are placed face down in a stack. Each player draws two cards to create a two-digit number then each makes her or his amount, using the fewest coins. In each round, the player using fewer coins receives a counter. The player with more counters after five rounds wins.

## Focus
▶ Use all four operations to solve word problems involving money, using one or more steps, including converting pounds to pence and vice versa.

**Player A**

5 7

"For 57p I need a 50p, 5p and 2p coin. That's three coins. I win!"

**Player B**

1 9

"For 19p I need a 10p, 5p and two 2p coins. That's four coins. I lose!"

### Assessment Tip:
▶ Does the child count mixed coins with ease?

# Product Comparing

## Materials
One set of 0–9 numeral cards, 5 counters, paper, a penny

## Directions
Players flip a coin to determine whether the game is a "greater than" or "less than" game. Heads means "greater than," and tails means "less than." The players use this to determine who will win each round, with the winner receiving a counter.

Numeral cards are spread out face down. Each player draws four cards and arranges them into a 2-digit by 1-digit multiplication problem, discarding the card that seems least helpful. Players compute the products, then **read them using the language of comparison. (One hundred and twenty is less than four hundred and sixty-eight.)** The comparisons are recorded on the paper, using the <, >, and = symbols.

At the end of five rounds, the player with more counters wins.

## Variations
1. Draw 5 cards and require 1-digit by 3-digit multiplication.
2. Draw 5 cards and require 2-digit by 2-digit multiplication.

## Focus
▶ Solve mathematical problems or puzzles, recognise and explain patterns and relationships, generalise and predict, suggest extensions by asking "What if …?"

## Assessment Tips:
▶ Is the child developing strategies for placing the numerals to create the winning product?
▶ Is the child using mental maths strategies to compute products? If so, which strategies are being used?

# KEEP THE LEFTOVERS

## MATERIALS
Fifty beans or other counters, one 4–9 number dice, paper

## DIRECTIONS
Players create a recording sheet for each game like the one shown. The game begins with fifty beans. The first player rolls the dice, divides the current number of beans by that number, and **states the division.** (50 divided into groups of 8 is 6 groups of 8 with 2 left over.) The player takes the remainder in beans and **tells the other player how many beans to start with.** The game continues until no beans remain. The player with more beans wins.

## VARIATIONS
1. Start with a different number of beans.
2. Use a different dice to provide different divisors.
3. To help players become familiar with the concept of division as sharing, use the number on the dice to determine the number of groups among which to share the beans.

## FOCUS
▶ Express a remainder as a whole number.

Josh
50 ÷ 8 = 6 r ②

"50 divided into groups of 8 is 6 groups of 8 with a remainder of 2, so I get 2 beans. Since 6 groups of 8 are 48, you start with 48."

## ASSESSMENT TIP:
▶ Is the child using simple division facts with confidence in a situation where remainders are common?

**Partner Games: Year 4**

# MULTIPLICATION ARRAYS

### MATERIALS
Multiplication Array Game Board on page 22, 80 pennies (or 50 each of two distinct counters), one 1–6 number dice, one 4–9 number dice, paper

### DIRECTIONS
The object of the game is for players to create rectangular arrays of counters on the game board. Players make individual recording sheets as shown. Players take turns tossing the dice and laying out an array of pennies on the game board that matches the results of the toss. Players **describe the array and record the multiplication fact.** Once a circle has been included in an array, it is out of play. Play continues until each child has been unable to make an array for two turns. The player with more pennies on the game board wins.

### VARIATIONS
1. Use two 1–6 dice.
2. Have players circle and initial their arrays.

### FOCUS
▶ Know by heart multiplication facts for 2, 3, 4, 5 and 10 times-tables.
▶ Begin to know multiplication facts for 6, 7, 8 and 9 times-tables.

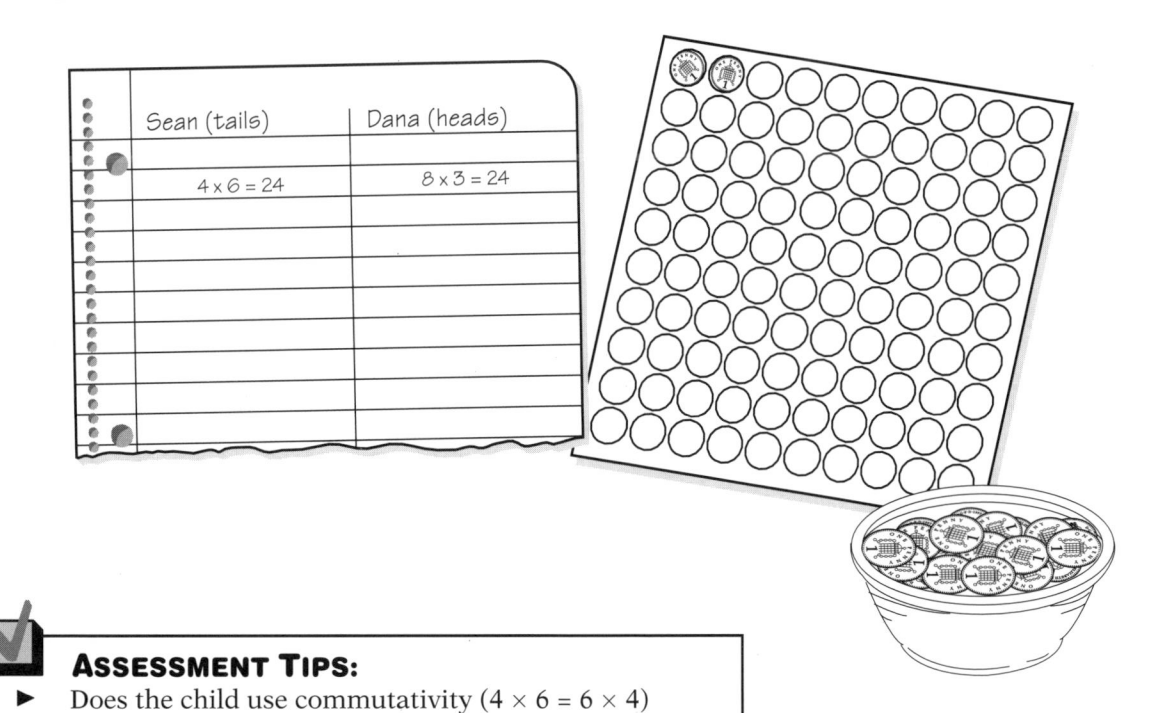

| Sean (tails) | Dana (heads) |
|---|---|
| 4 × 6 = 24 | 8 × 3 = 24 |

### ASSESSMENT TIPS:
▶ Does the child use commutativity (4 × 6 = 6 × 4) to help find a place on the board to fit an array?
▶ Is the child comfortable with the multiplication facts?

# Try for 10 000

## Materials
Base ten apparatus such as Dienes blocks (24 tens, 24 hundreds, and 19 thousands), one 1–6 number dice, paper

## Directions
The object of the game is to get as close to 10,000 as possible without going over. Players take turns tossing the dice and deciding whether to take that number in thousands, hundreds, or tens. Players record each toss on their papers and **state their running total.** Whenever possible, players exchange for the next-higher value block. After six tosses the player closer to 10 000 without going over wins.

## Variations
1. Allow 10 tosses of the dice.
2. Choose a different target total.
3. Use the 4–9 dice.

## Focus
▶ Read and write numbers to at least 10 000 in figure and words; know what each digit represents, and partition numbers into thousands, hundreds, tens and ones (TH H T U).

Name Caleb

| | thousands | hundreds | tens | ones |
|---|---|---|---|---|
| 1. | 1 | | | |
| 2. | | 6 | 0 | 0 |
| 3. | 6 | 0 | 0 | 0 |
| 4. | | | 0 | 0 |
| 5. | | 5 | 0 | 0 |
| 6. | | | | |

"Wow, I'm close to 10 000 and I still have two turns left. I'll need to choose carefully!"

### Assessment Tips:
▶ Does the child have a strategy for choosing the value of blocks to take on each turn?
▶ Does the child exchange for the next-higher block at appropriate times?
▶ Is the child comfortable with mental addition?

**Partner Games: Year 4**

# Big double trouble

## Materials
One 1–6 number dice, one 4–9 number dice, paper, calculator (optional)

## Focus
▶ Develop standard written methods for column addition and subtraction for: HTU ± HT

## Directions
The goal is to be the first player to reach 1000. The first player tosses the dice, states the sum, then multiplies the sum by 10. He or she then records the number, and continues to toss and list each number until he or she either chooses to end the turn or tosses a double. Tossing a double results in a loss of all the sums listed for that turn. When a player chooses to end a turn, the sums are added and recorded and the total for play to this point is circled. Players take turns until one player's total reaches or exceeds 1000.

## Variation
1. If the player who wins was the player who started the game, the other player has one more "fair" turn to reach or surpass the first player's total.
2. Players may want to use calculators for the column addition required to add the sums.
3. Multiply the sum by 20 with 2000 as the goal.

## Assessment Tips:
▶ Does the child add multiples of ten as comfortably as simple facts?
▶ Does the child have mental maths strategies for addition?
▶ How does the child determine when to end his or her turn?

Copyright © Thomas Nelson and Sons Ltd 1999

Partner Games: Year 4

# Counting Tape Game

### MATERIALS
Counting Tape Game Board on page 23, one 1–6 number dice, 2 counters or other markers, calculator, paper

### DIRECTIONS
Counters are placed in the 'Start' box. Players take turns tossing the dice. The current player may move to the *next* space that is a multiple of the number on the dice (that is, the next number that can be divided evenly by the number on the dice). The player then **tells his or her opponent the number sentence that justifies the move.** (Three times seventeen is fifty-one.) The opponent may challenge and check with a calculator. The first player to land exactly on the 'End' box wins.

### VARIATIONS
1. Create a new Counting Tape Game Board with different numbers.
2. Use the 4–9 dice.

### FOCUS
▶ Derive quickly division facts corresponding to 2, 3, 4, 5 and 10 times-tables.

**Counting Tape Game Board**

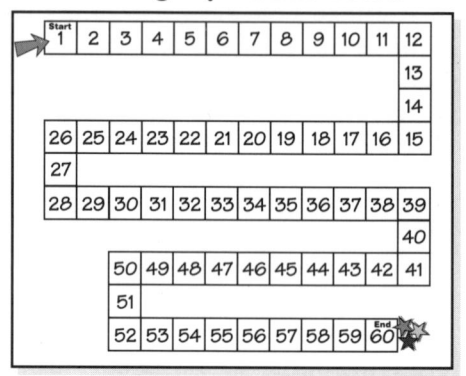

| Start 1 | 2 | 3 | 4 | 5 | 6 | 7 | 8 | 9 | 10 | 11 | 12 |
|---|---|---|---|---|---|---|---|---|---|---|---|
|  |  |  |  |  |  |  |  |  |  |  | 13 |
|  |  |  |  |  |  |  |  |  |  |  | 14 |
| 26 | 25 | 24 | 23 | 22 | 21 | 20 | 19 | 18 | 17 | 16 | 15 |
| 27 |  |  |  |  |  |  |  |  |  |  |  |
| 28 | 29 | 30 | 31 | 32 | 33 | 34 | 35 | 36 | 37 | 38 | 39 |
|  |  |  |  |  |  |  |  |  |  |  | 40 |
|  | 50 | 49 | 48 | 47 | 46 | 45 | 44 | 43 | 42 | 41 |  |
|  | 51 |  |  |  |  |  |  |  |  |  |  |
|  | 52 | 53 | 54 | 55 | 56 | 57 | 58 | 59 | End 60 |  |  |

### ASSESSMENT TIP:
▶ Does the child use mental maths strategies to define a move?

Partner Games: Year 4

Copyright © Thomas Nelson and Sons Ltd 1999

# Make a Whole

## Materials
Make a Whole Game Board on page 24, pencil, paper clip, coloured crayons, spinner below

## Directions
The object is to be the first to create a combination of fractional parts to equal one whole. The first player spins a paper clip round the spinner below, using a pencil to hold it at the centre, and reads the fraction. The player colours the fraction on their game board, and **and tells the total. (I have three-quarters.)** If a player cannot use the fraction, he or she loses the turn. The first player to fill in the whole wins.

## Focus
▶ Recognise the equivalence of simple fractions.

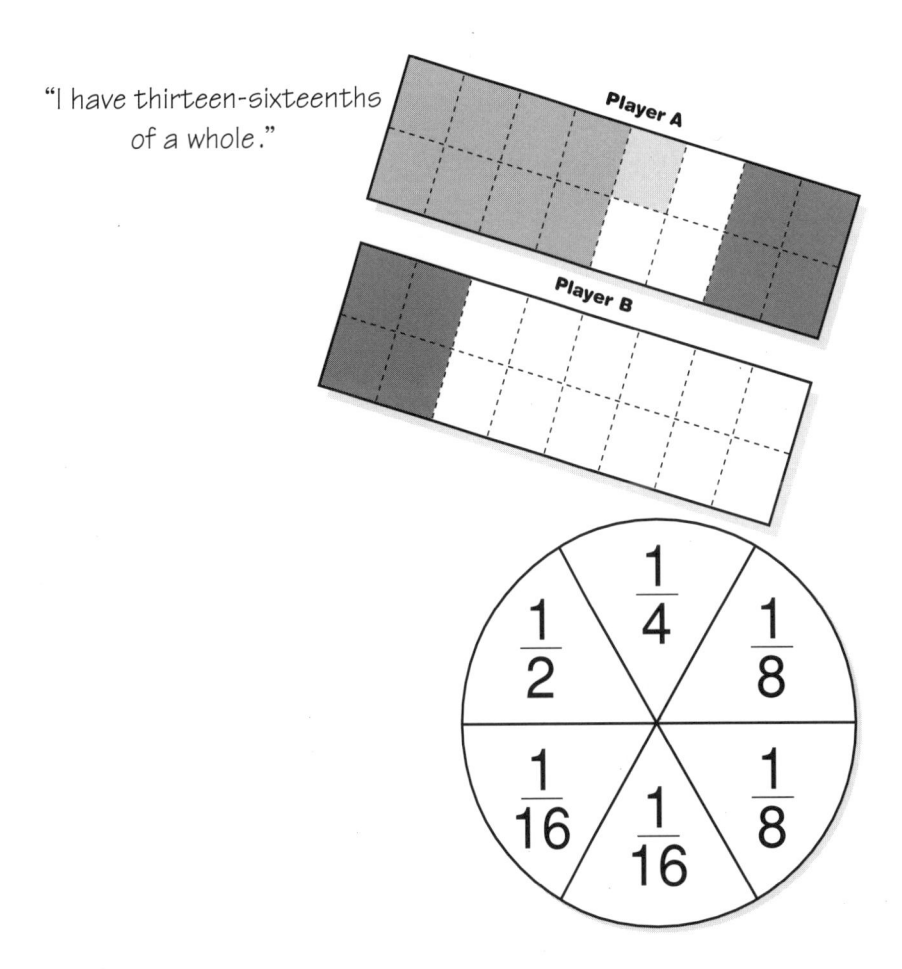

"I have thirteen-sixteenths of a whole."

### Assessment Tip:
▶ Is the child able to read the fraction that is coloured?

Copyright © Thomas Nelson and Sons Ltd 1999

**Partner Games: Year 4**

# Multiple Marker Game

## Materials
Multiple Maker Game Board on page 25, twenty of each of blue, red, green, yellow and black counters, paper

## Directions
The object is for a player to place four counters in a row. The blue can be placed on multiples of 2, the red on multiples of 3, the green on multiples of 4, the yellow on multiples of 5, and the black on multiples of 6. Players take turns placing counters on the board and **telling why the counter belongs in that place. (I'll put a blue on the 20 because 10 x 2 is 20. 20 is a multiple of 2.)** Players have ten of each colour of counter. The first player to place the last of four counters in a row wins the game.

## Focus
▶ Know by heart multiplication facts for 2, 3, 4, 5 and 10 times-tables.
▶ Begin to know multiplication facts for 6, 7, 8 and 9 times-tables.

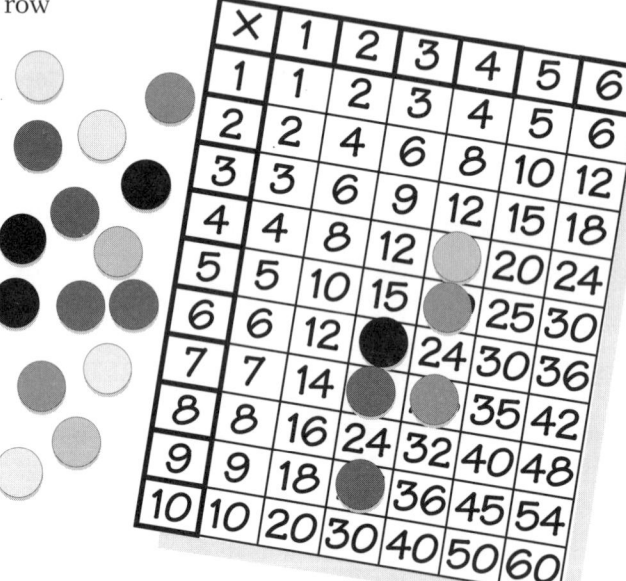

## Assessment Tips:
▶ Does the child devise strategies both for winning and for blocking the opponent?
▶ Is the child comfortable with the concepts of multiples and factors?

Partner Games: Year 4

Copyright © Thomas Nelson and Sons Ltd 1999

# METRE STICK RACE

## MATERIALS
Metre stick, one 1–6 number dice, one 4–9 number dice, two paper clips

## DIRECTIONS
Each player straightens a paper clip to make a pointer. To start, pointers are placed at the 0 point on either side of the metre stick. The object of the game is to be the first player to reach the 100 point on the metre stick.

Players take turns tossing the dice and moving ahead the number of centimetres that is equal to their sum. **Each player must state the sum and predict the result of the move.** (For example, 7 centimetres added to my 45 centimetres will put me at 52 centimetres. That's point 52 of a metre.) The first player to reach the end of the metre stick with an exact toss of the dice wins.

## VARIATION
Use two 1–6 dice.

## FOCUS
▶ Use decimal notation in context: for example, convert a length such as 125 cm to metres.

---

**ASSESSMENT TIPS:**
▶ Does the child use whole-number facts to help compute decimal sums?
▶ Does the child make strategic choices?

Copyright © Thomas Nelson and Sons Ltd 1999

Partner Games: Year 4

# Fraction/Decimal Cover Up

## Materials
One pack of Fraction/Decimal Cards without the cards greater than one-quarter, 10 × 10 Grids Game Board on page 26, dried beans or other small counters (200)

## Directions
Shuffle the pack, placing the cards face down in a stack between the players. Players take turns turning over the top card from the pack, **stating the number.** The player then uses the beans to cover the portion of his or her game board equal to the amount on the card. Before taking another turn the player must **state the amount of the game board that is covered as either a decimal or a fraction.** The first player to cover the game board completely wins.

## Variations
1. At the end of each round, compare and record the amounts covered on the grids using <, >, =.
2. At the start of each round, players verbalise the amount needed to completely cover their grids. (I have thirty-five hundredths. I need sixty-five hundredths.)

## Focus
▶ Recognise the equivalence between the decimal and fraction forms of one half, one quarter and one tenth.

## Assessment Tip:
▶ Does the child have good benchmarks for equivalent fractions and fraction/decimal equivalents?
▶ Can the child read and interpret fractions and decimals?

# Fraction/Decimal Concentration

## Materials
One pack of Fraction/Decimal Cards

## Directions
A player shuffles the cards and arranges them face down in a 7 × 7 array. Players take turns turning over two cards, **reading them, and comparing them. (I have twenty-five hundredths and one quarter; twenty-five hundredths equals one quarter.)** When a player turns over two cards of equal value, he or she keeps the cards. Any match — fraction to decimal, fraction to fraction, or decimal to decimal — counts. If there is no match, the cards are returned face down to their places in the array and play continues. The first player to win ten cards wins the game.

## Variation
To reinforce fractions, play only with the fraction cards.

## Focus
▶ Recognise the equivalence between the decimal and fraction forms of one half, one quarter and one tenth.

### Assessment Tip:
▶ Does the child have decimal benchmarks for halves, quarters, and fifths?

Copyright © Thomas Nelson and Sons Ltd 1999

Partner Games: Year 4

# From Here to There Fractions

## Materials
One 1–6 number dice, one 4–9 number dice, Fractions Recording Sheet on page 28

## Directions
The object of the game is to try to write fractions from smallest to largest. Each player has a copy of the Fractions Recording Sheet. Players take turns rolling the two dice to create a fraction. After **stating the fraction, the player decides where to write the fraction on the recording sheet.** If a player is unable to write a fraction in an empty square, the player loses that turn. Play continues until one player has filled in the recording sheet and proves that the sequence of fractions is from smallest to largest.

## Variations
1. Order the fractions from greatest to least.
2. Players illustrate each fraction before placing it on the recording sheet.
3. Players toss two 1–6 dice and use the results to create fractions smaller than 1.

## Focus
▶ Use fraction notation; recognise simple fractions that are several parts of a whole such as $\frac{2}{3}$ or $\frac{5}{8}$.

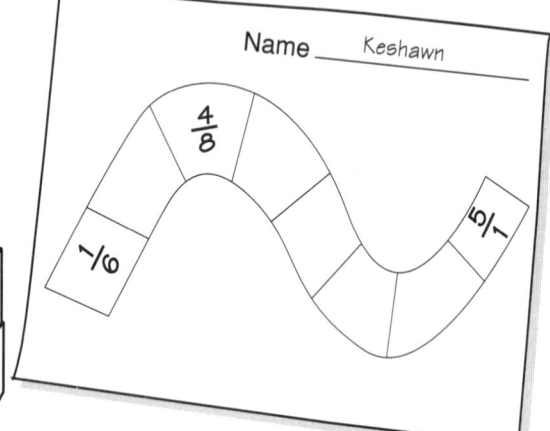

## Assessment Tips:
▶ Does the child write the fractions on the recording sheet randomly or with careful thought?
▶ Has the child thought about the smallest possible fraction and the largest possible fraction that can be created with the dice?
▶ In writing the fractions on the path, what fraction sense is demonstrated by the child?

Partner Games: Year 4

# FIGURING FACTORS

### MATERIALS
Figuring Factors Game Board on page 27, one 1–6 number dice, 10 counters, calculator, paper

### DIRECTIONS
Players create recording sheets as shown. They take turns tossing the dice. The player places a counter on a number on the board that is a multiple of the number on the dice. The covered number may not be used again in this game. He or she then **names and records as many factors for that number as possible.** The player receives one point for each correct factor. The opponent may challenge any named factor, checking its accuracy with the calculator. After each player has taken five turns, the player with more points wins.

### VARIATIONS
1. Create a new Figuring Factors Game Board with different numbers.
2. Use the 4–9 dice.

### FOCUS
▶ Solve mathematical problems or puzzles, recognise and explain patterns and relationships, generalise and predict; suggest extensions by asking "What if …?"

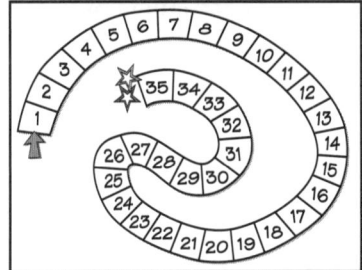

*I'll cover the 6 because its factors are 1, 2, 3, and 6. I get 4 points.*

### ASSESSMENT TIP:
▶ Can the child identify the prime numbers and numbers that have several factors and use this knowledge to form strategies for winning?

# Quotient Comparing

## Materials
2–9 numeral cards, 5 counters; paper

## Directions
The object of the game is to get the larger quotient. The Numeral Cards are spread out face down. Each player draws four cards and arranges them into a 2-digit by 1-digit division problem, discarding the card that seems least helpful. Players compute the quotients, then **read them using the language of comparison.** (Fifteen with a remainder of 2 is greater than three with a remainder of 1.) The comparisons are recorded on the paper, using the <, >, and = symbols.

The player with the greater quotient receives a counter for the round. At the end of five rounds, the player with more counters wins.

## Variations
1. Use base ten apparatus or money to act out the division.
2. Draw five cards and require 3-digit by 1-digit division.
3. Draw six cards and require 4-digit by 1-digit division.

## Focus
▶ Use the relationship between multiplication and division.
▶ Use, read and write the vocabulary of comparing and ordering numbers; use correct symbols such as <, >, =; give one or more numbers lying between two others and order a set of whole numbers with up to four digits.

|   | John | Amy |
|---|---|---|
| 1. | 351 ÷ 4 = 87r3 < | 297 ÷ 3 = 99 |
| 2. | | |
| 3. | | |
| 4. | | |
| 5. | | |

### Assessment Tips:
▶ Is the child developing strategies for placing the numerals to create the appropriate quotient?
▶ Is the child using mental maths strategies to compute?

# TOTAL 100

## MATERIALS
Total 100 Game Board on page 29, 70 blue and 70 red counters, two pack of 0 to 9 numeral cards, a stop clock

## DIRECTIONS
Partners decide who will use red and who will use blue counters. Shuffle the cards, and place them face down on the table. Players take turns to draw two cards, make a tens and units number, and find the partner number to total 100. (I have made 67; 67 and 33 equals 100.) They cover both numbers with counters on the game board. They start the stop clock at the beginning of their turn, and must cover the two numbers within ten seconds. If they do not find the answer within ten seconds they lose a turn. The winner is the one with the most counters on the game board.

## VARIATIONS
1. Write each pair as an addition sum.
2. Make two 2-digit numbers from each draw of the cards (67 and 76) and find and cover both sets of pairs to make 100 within twenty seconds.

## FOCUS
▶ Derive quickly all number pairs that total 100.

## ASSESSMENT TIP:
▶ Does the child count up from the smaller number to 100 to find the difference?

## MULTIPLICATION ARRAY GAME BOARD

Partner Games: Year 4

## COUNTING TAPE GAME BOARD

| Start 1 | 2 | 3 | 4 | 5 | 6 | 7 | 8 | 9 | 10 | 11 | 12 |
|---|---|---|---|---|---|---|---|---|---|---|---|

| 13 | 14 | 15 |
|---|---|---|
| | | 16 |
| | | 17 |
| | | 18 |
| | | 19 |
| 21 | 20 | |
| 22 | | |
| 23 | | |
| 24 | | |
| 25 | | |
| 26 | | |
| 27 | | |
| 28 | 29 | 30 | 31 | 32 | 33 | 34 | 35 | 36 | 37 | 38 | 39 |

| 40 | 41 |
| 42 |
| 43 |
| 44 |
| 45 |
| 46 |
| 47 |
| 48 |
| 49 | 50 |
| 51 |
| 52 | 53 | 54 | 55 | 56 | 57 | 58 | 59 | End 60 |

**Partner Games: Year 4**

23

## MAKE A WHOLE GAME BOARD

**Player A**

**Player B**

Partner Games: Year 4

Copyright © Thomas Nelson and Sons Ltd 1999

## MULTIPLE MARKER GAME BOARD

| ×  | 1  | 2  | 3  | 4  | 5  | 6  |
|----|----|----|----|----|----|----|
| 1  | 1  | 2  | 3  | 4  | 5  | 6  |
| 2  | 2  | 4  | 6  | 8  | 10 | 12 |
| 3  | 3  | 6  | 9  | 12 | 15 | 18 |
| 4  | 4  | 8  | 12 | 16 | 20 | 24 |
| 5  | 5  | 10 | 15 | 20 | 25 | 30 |
| 6  | 6  | 12 | 18 | 24 | 30 | 36 |
| 7  | 7  | 14 | 21 | 28 | 35 | 42 |
| 8  | 8  | 16 | 24 | 32 | 40 | 48 |
| 9  | 9  | 18 | 27 | 36 | 45 | 54 |
| 10 | 10 | 20 | 30 | 40 | 50 | 60 |

# 10 X 10 GRIDS GAME BOARD

**Player B**

**Player A**

Partner Games: Year 4

Copyright © Thomas Nelson and Sons Ltd 1999

## FIGURING FACTORS GAME BOARD

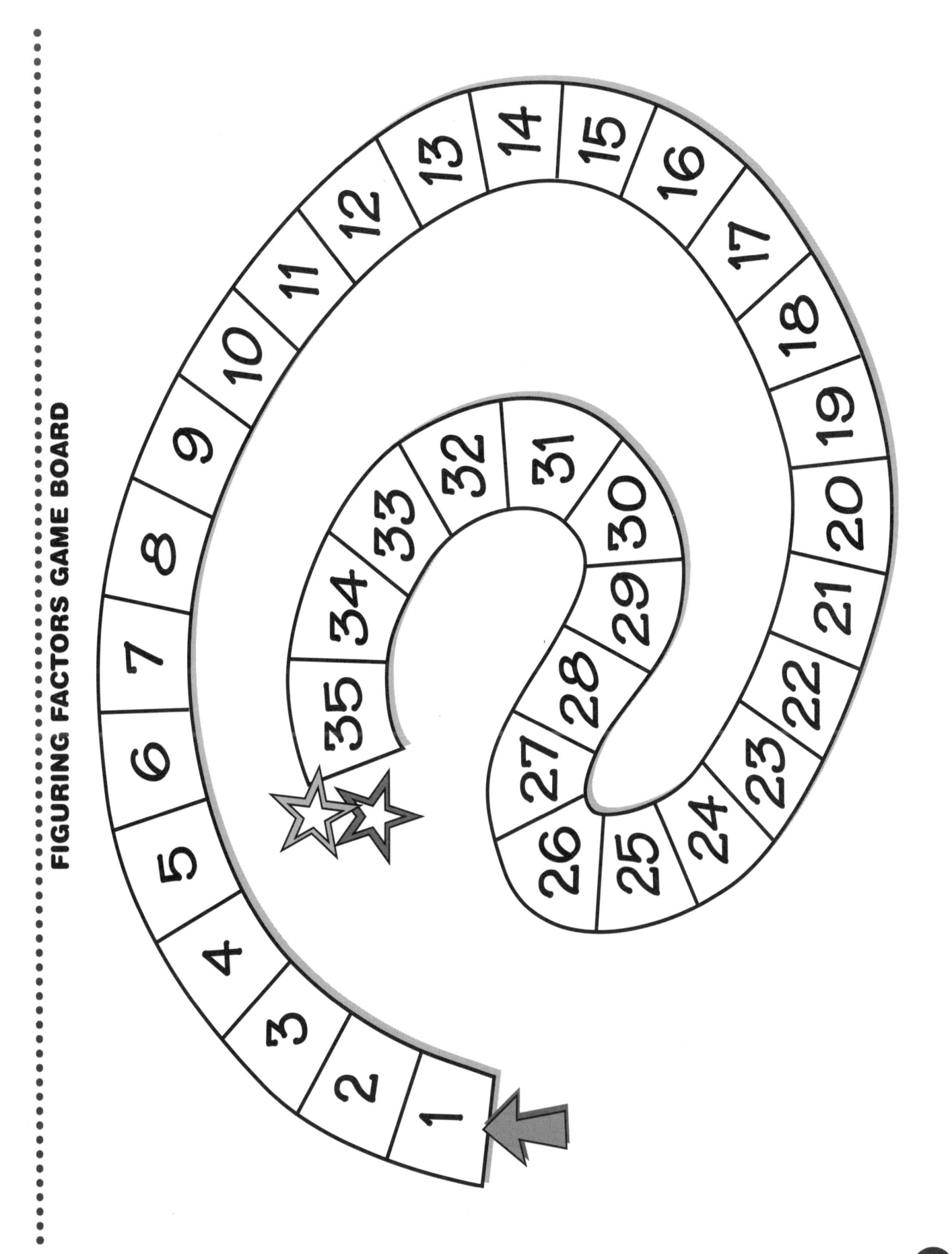

Copyright © Thomas Nelson and Sons Ltd 1999

Partner Games: Year 4

# FRACTIONS RECORDING SHEET

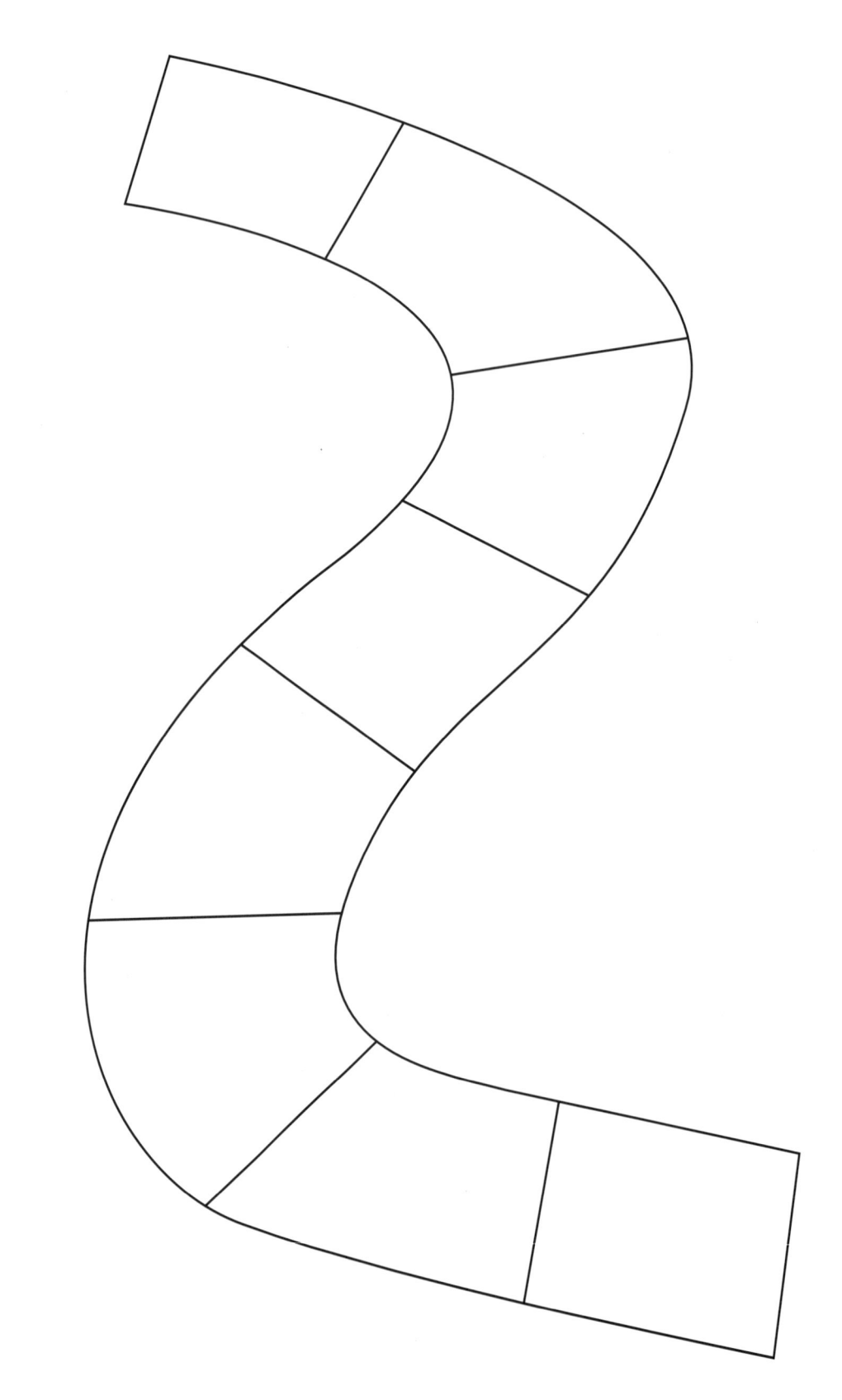

Name _____

Partner Games: Year 4

Copyright © Thomas Nelson and Sons Ltd 1999

## TOTAL 100 GAME BOARD

| 1 | 2 | 3 | 4 | 5 | 6 | 7 | 8 | 9 | 10 |
|---|---|---|---|---|---|---|---|---|---|
| 11 | 12 | 13 | 14 | 15 | 16 | 17 | 18 | 19 | 20 |
| 21 | 22 | 23 | 24 | 25 | 26 | 27 | 28 | 29 | 30 |
| 31 | 32 | 33 | 34 | 35 | 36 | 37 | 38 | 39 | 40 |
| 41 | 42 | 43 | 44 | 45 | 46 | 47 | 48 | 49 | 50 |
| 51 | 52 | 53 | 54 | 55 | 56 | 57 | 58 | 59 | 60 |
| 61 | 62 | 63 | 64 | 65 | 66 | 67 | 68 | 69 | 70 |
| 71 | 72 | 73 | 74 | 75 | 76 | 77 | 78 | 79 | 80 |
| 81 | 82 | 83 | 84 | 85 | 86 | 87 | 88 | 89 | 90 |
| 91 | 92 | 93 | 94 | 95 | 96 | 97 | 98 | 99 | 100 |